It's Me, O Lord

New Prayers for Every Day

Illustrated by Paul Shuttleworth

IT'S ME,
O LORD

By MICHAEL HOLLINGS
and ETTA GULLICK

Hodder and Stoughton
London Sydney Auckland Toronto

Contents

CONTENTS

CONTENTS

CONTENTS

CONTENTS

Foreword

IT SEEMS, in some ways, a funny idea to produce these prayers, but we were asked to do so, so here they are!

We would like to thank Frances Makower for writing some of the prayers on illness and Bertha Maude and Monique Raffray for prayers on examinations, and John Hooper and David Braine for helpful criticism and suggestions on the prayers which we have written.

We personally can only pray that the Spirit of the Lord will be with you, and ask, whatever your reactions to these pages are, that you will pray for us.

ETTA GULLICK
MICHAEL HOLLINGS

Conversion of Saint Paul 1972

I

It's Me, O Lord

THIS is a book of informal prayers connected with daily life and the situations we find there, with our moods and feelings about people, our situation in the world.

Human life has so many aspects. And there are so many things that prayer is too; for God, the all-powerful, can transform human living beyond our imagination if we let him.

The whole of life can be lived with God. It is the most natural thing in the world to cry out to God during the day and for different reasons. Prayers can be made in many words, in short sentences, in a single word, a glance, a sigh, a silence. Prayers may be superficial, made on a surface level, or so deep as to involve our whole being.

The important thing about prayer is that it is almost indefinable. You see, it is:

hard and sharp

soft and loving   deep and inexpressible

shallow and repetitious   a groaning and a sighing

a silence and a shouting

a burst of praise

digging deep down into loneliness, into me

loving

abandonment to despair

a soaring to heights which can be only ecstasy

dull plodding in the greyness of mediocre being

laziness

boredom

resentment

questing and questioning

calm reflection

meditation

cogitation

a surprise at sudden joy

a shaft of light   a laser beam

irritation at not understanding   impatience

pain of mind and body hardly uttered or deeply anguished

being together

the stirring of love shallow, then deeper, then deepest

a breathless involvement

a meeting

a longing

a loving   an impouring

a drowning

a swooning

more*

* Our publisher originally told us that this layout would look messy and chaotic. We said: "Fine, that's just what prayer-life is."

So how can anyone help anyone else? Surely you can only experience prayer yourself, not through anyone else?

Well, we think and feel (can you forgive the words and try to grasp what is behind them?) each in so many ways because we are so many differing individuals.

The message behind this book is simply this:

No man is an island. I am of the community of man —and—I AM UNIQUE.

From this it follows that now and then I come across something written, spoken, or thought by another and it makes me exclaim: (using my silly colloquial phrase) "That rings a bell with me". You know what I mean?

I am unique, but I am human. I share the common heritage of man with its moods, feelings, depths which range over comedy, tragedy, mediocrity. I may find my experiences, my feelings reflected in the Psalms, in the book of Job, throughout the Bible, because the psalmist, Job, the men and women of the New and Old Testaments were uniquely themselves before God. They were not afraid to say "it's me" and to tell the Lord what they thought of their predicament, his treatment of them and their world. They were shocking and outrageous at times—no doubt startling to the pious of their day—but they were fully themselves before God. They spoke in everyday language to the Lord and spoke to him as a friend.

I am to be like the psalmist, like the prophets, and to

have, at times, shocking views and feelings like theirs about life, to have thoughts that are far from nice! I, too, can lay my problems and situations honestly and fearlessly before God as his friends have done through the ages. He will be in my situation as he was with the men and women of the Old and New Testaments, for I am his and belong to the community of man too. You see talking to God naturally and honestly is not new but it is also *for now*.

In these pages, you will find a whole series of expressions which we have felt and thought, or which have been "fed" to us by others. They move from the sublime to the ridiculous, and rightly so, because we are living the human experience.

Is there anything more sublime than two people in love with each other, or someone caught up in the love of God? Is there anything more ridiculous than a human being shaking his fist at God, or telling a petty lie just to save face?

As human beings, you and I run the whole course of life from youth to age, touching so many situations and emotions. No one of us has been this way before, but perhaps another has, or glimpsed the other side of the hill you are climbing. So we hope that what we have touched here in prayer may somewhere, somehow, sometime touch you. Or, it may help you to express through our words what you feel.

But, better still, we hope that what you meet here will encourage you to meet God without fear, to be with God, to talk to God, to learn to experience your own thing in your own way, in words or in silence, emptiness or fullness, so that when you go to pray as well as in daily life you can express quite simply (and you may very well use different words!)—

It's me, O Lord!

II

The Need of Prayer

IT's ME, O Lord, full of contradictions; I have loving and hating thoughts and feelings about you and my neighbours. I am unbelieving and yet I believe. I have sublime thoughts about you, but when things go wrong I swear and blame you for everything. I want to love you more, to adore you and to love others, but so often things get in the way, particularly things I think important and things I want. Lord, increase my faith and love, and help me to put the self-centred me on one side so that you may enter more fully into my life and make me more like Jesus. Lord, never leave me, and give me your precious gift of hope, especially the hope of living for ever with you. Amen.

When unbelieving

HERE I am, Lord, finding it very hard to believe that you exist. I realize that I may be saying this into a void, but though I disbelieve with my mind, some other part of me recognizes in a dim way that you exist. Then I wonder if this half-intuition is wishful thinking. I am in a great confusion! All I can say is: Lord, if you exist, help my unbelief and inspire me to go on trying to find you.

Belief

SOMETIMES it seems silly to say I love you, Lord, because I've never seen you, and I don't know you as I know an ordinary human being. Yet I experience you in a strange deep way which is very close and wonderful. So, I can't help loving you in yourself, quietly and radiantly; and in your creation too. I can't quite explain this to anyone, but sometimes somebody else simply knows what I mean. This is wonderful and strengthening, and it makes me understand that I am right if I go on saying I love you.

Self-offering

LORD, here I am, do what you want with me. I am not much use, not very intelligent, not virtuous or good-looking, but all that I am I offer to you. Take me, come into the heart of my being, diffuse your love through all my life. Help me to be always open to you however much I want to be doing my own thing and not yours, dear Lord.

III

Prayers for the Beginning of the Day

LORD, give me strength today to live as you would like me to, without fear, joyfully and lovingly. Help me not to get flustered and agitated when things go wrong, and when there is confusion and tension. Give me your deep peace so that I can remain calm whatever happens, and in this way help others, too, to turn to you for strength and support, for the sake of Jesus our Lord.

LORD, I am dreading today. It's going to be very busy, and I am going to have to deal with some difficult people. If I stand up to them as I ought, it will be very unpleasant. Please give me the courage to do what is right even if it makes me disliked. Help me to bear any hurt which I may receive without crumpling up and giving in to my misery. Be before me as an example, and make me realize that you are with me in all my difficulties, today and always.

LIVING close to you, Lord, there is a certain sense of quiet anticipation as I wake in the morning: a mixture of buoyancy and hope, of the knowledge of loving and being loved, of excitement about what the day will bring. Of course Lord, it is often filled with dread at some difficult situation. But it is good to be alive, to get up and be with you in prayer—to go out into your world, to meet your people and to know you love us. Teach me today to love more fully.

JESUS, I am sure that today I will become so involved in my daily activities that I will often forget you. When this happens, please never stop remembering me and being with me. In your daily life on earth you never forgot your Father; please help me, in some way or other, to live in a continual awareness of his presence as you did.

I LOVE to wake in the morning before it is time to get up, Lord. Then I can lie there, relaxed, unhurried, realizing your presence in a deep and often bubbling kind of joy. How wonderful you are. I love waking up now. Thank you.

IV
Prayers About Daily Life

When my car is run into

LORD, I'm hopping mad; that man's crashed into my car. Stop me from telling him what I think of him! It won't do any good to let fly at him, but I want to. Lord, why can't you keep fools like him off the road?

Passenger's prayer

O GOD, please help me to keep calm and not to worry when I am being driven by someone else who seems to go too fast, and who does not appear to anticipate what other drivers will do and at the last moment slams on the brake. Stop me from being fussed and agitated. And help me to trust and to find rest and peace in you so that I may pray for others and forget myself as I travel along.

Driver's prayer

PROTECT me as I travel by road, and guard me from danger and hurt. Make me drive carefully and with consideration for others, and stop me from injuring others. Prevent me from being bad-tempered when the traffic goes slowly, and help me realize that delays can afford us opportunities for turning to you. Help me to be alert and attentive, and to remember that others can be in a hurry too, and my impatience can infuriate them!

Praying in a train (bus)

LORD, here I am on this train (bus) with time to pray, but it is very crowded and noisy and I am finding it difficult to concentrate. Please help me to keep turning to you even though my mind gets frequently taken up with other things or people. I know the people can become part of my prayer and I do pray that they may come to love you; but could you show me another way of praying in a crowd? A way which will help me to be rooted firmly in you whatever the noise and bustle of life, so that I may sense that you are always with me.

I sit in the train and try to pray, Lord. Give me patience with that person chattering over there. And I ask, Lord, should I be chattering too? Somehow spreading your love instead of glowering at that noisy kid? Teach me through people in the train, Lord, how to love my neighbour as myself.

Thanksgiving in a train

I SAT in the train, Lord. We were going along the coast. It was autumn and everything was dazzling in the sun-

You are the Lord of joy and hope

Please cheer up your people

light—the green of field, the blue of sea, the golden tints of trees—so lovely I felt I could burst, and all of it your creation! Thank you for so very much.

In a slow-moving train

LORD, it is wonderful to rest quietly in you and with you as I travel along in a slow-moving train. You fill me with love and peace and I am very grateful to you. Please make this peace grow in me and underlie all my other activities today.

Trying to find God in a crowd travelling to work

I SUPPOSE you're in this crowd that is going off to work, Lord. It's drab and grey, doesn't seem human, let alone divine. I remember that they wrote of you that you emptied yourself and became a man. This is pretty emptying, Lord! Will you let me learn how it may be full, how you may come among us again in my emptiness?

Waiting in an airport

LORD, I am afraid. Sixty people were killed in an air crash yesterday. Now I am thinking of all the things that could go wrong with the plane, knowing so well that there would be nothing that I could do about it. An engine could catch fire, and—I know it's stupid, but a wing could drop off, so many things could happen. Give me courage, help me not to worry, and make me see if I get killed today I am in your hands. However, Lord, I don't want to die at this moment as I enjoy life so much, so please keep this plane safe!

The take-off of a jet plane

LORD, I am exhilarated by the speed of the take-off. I am thrilled and the joy of it makes me sing in praise to you. I thank you for the skill of the men who make and pilot these great machines. It is wonderful! Lord, do not let me forget those who are afraid of flying; make me sympathetic towards them, and not contemptuous and superior. Please comfort them and help them to turn to you for courage.

On the plane

IT's a long flight, Lord, and rather dull. But there is so much to learn—the other passengers, the children. How patient the stewardesses are as people push past and get in the way. Then the going up and coming down, the flight above the clouds, your nature, Lord, and its glory. I think of the power of man and his skill in flying, and then his weakness and the mess we make. Help us to live our lives safely under your care, Lord of the Universe.

Fear of going home at night

I AM dead scared, Lord! They have been lying in wait and beating people up as they go home at night. Give me courage, Lord, and protect me. I'm so very much afraid of that walk tonight.

Housework

LORD, housework is so boring. I do the same dusting and sweeping every day. It seems so futile. I would much prefer to do something to help people who are in trouble and suffering, but I have to do this. I know that I should do it willingly as your will, and that I ought to pray for others and praise you as I work, but this seems so insignificant. Help me, Lord, not to be proud and to do this work gladly for you. Make me realize that praying for others, too, is part of the work you want me to do, and pray with me.

Asking forgiveness on the spot

LORD, I have just told a lie. I did it without thinking (did it deliberately). I hate myself for having done this. I was afraid my inefficiency would be shown up. Lord, I am very sorry and humbly ask you to forgive me. I know you forgive me immediately when I am sorry, but somehow it is right that I should ask forgiveness in words. Help me not to sin like this again. Give me strength, for of myself I can do nothing. I ask this, Lord, for your sake.

Washing up

LORD, I enjoy cooking. It's creative and interesting, but

washing up afterwards on my own is hateful. The pots are clogged, the plates are greasy, and there seems so much of it. If the rest of the family helped it would be different—it would be companionable and happy. Lord, I am disheartened. Help me to get through it without being grumpy and feeling a martyr.

Looking for something lost

LORD, I am always losing things. I know it is my own fault as I am untidy. I always say: "Lord, if you help me to find what I am looking for, I will be more tidy," but somehow I keep on being in a muddle. You said: "Seek and you shall find." Well, Lord, I am seeking, now help me to find! Then, Lord, give me strength to try to be a little tidier so that I may not waste so much time looking for things!

I know I put it there, Lord, and yet it isn't there. Has someone taken it? I've only got a short time, and I must find it, please. Make my eyes see or my brain click, or something. And I'm so cross when this happens, especially now. Calm me, Lord, and teach me at the same time how blind I am and how little I see.

Alone in the house

LORD JESUS, I am alone and it is dark and I am afraid. The floorboards creak and the furniture groans, and I keep thinking there is someone moving about in the house. Lord, help me, take away my fear; make me realize that you are with me and so I never need be

39

afraid whatever happens, for you are Lord of all. Let me know you are with me; help me to feel your strength, and make me more trusting, dear Lord.

Miss World

I SPENT some of the evening watching the Miss World contest, Lord. You made the beauty of the female body. And there's so much variety of loveliness, but I wonder if you meant it to be paraded like that. Lovely as beauty is, it's only skin deep. And these lovely forms are real people, aren't they, Lord? And they know love and have rights. Teach me to respect the other, not just to exploit what you have made.

Sport

LORD, help us to realize that sport is for relaxation and life won't end if the other side wins. Help us to play fairly and obey the rules, and if possible to beat the others. If we lose let us accept defeat cheerfully; keep us from being bad-tempered and spiteful, and from spoiling the enjoyment of others.

An unsporting prayer

LORD, I want my team (or myself) to win this match and would like your help. Though it may not seem very important, it matters a great deal to me. I know I should want the best team to win, and shouldn't mind what happens because it is just a game, but I don't feel that way at all. So please help me if I get bad-tempered if we lose and get furious with you about the result.

Football pools

GIVE me a chance, Lord. Whose side are you on? Other people win the pools, so . . . what about me for a change?

Waiting for a boy friend/girl friend

LORD, I've been waiting ten minutes and he hasn't turned up. Am I at the right place? Make him come soon, don't let him forget. Lord, I am so afraid he has got tired of me. Please don't let this happen. Lord, I am agitated. Make me calm so that I look happy when he comes, and not put out and disgruntled.

Waiting for a telephone call

I'VE been waiting all afternoon for a telephone call, Lord. It is rather important to me. But because I'm waiting everything else gets unclear: I can't settle down or go out or do anything properly. It is silly to mind so much and to get so caught up. If only I could be more detached, Lord, and get on with what I have to do.

In a dentist's waiting room

DEAR LORD, I've a lot of things to get done and here I am in the dentist's waiting room—waiting! It's quite frustrating! I don't mind the pain of having my teeth drilled; it's a temporary pain and ends quite quickly, but this waiting can easily go on for an hour as I well know. Please help me to be patient and to realize that there will be time for the things that should be done; and if there isn't, make others tolerant of my failure to keep up.

I'm not very good at waiting, Lord, especially at the dentist's; my teeth get on edge and I think of the sound and the feel of the drill. I'm a coward about it. Can I offer it up? It's no good asking not to mind really —that would be too easy and there'd always be another time! So, Lord, let me wait patiently and not fidget.

Patience when waiting

LORD, give me patience when I have to wait for a bus, wait in a queue, wait to see the doctor or dentist, wait for the telephone line to be free. Stop me from feeling frustrated, angry, or agitated about being late. Make me see that waiting affords an opportunity for turning to you, of praying to you for others or for myself. Help me to realize that all time is in your hands, and that no time spent waiting with you is wasted.

Waiting for a daughter returning from school

LORD, keep my daughter safe. She is so late coming back from school and I am dreadfully afraid. She may have been run over, or someone may have picked her up. Please let it be neither of these things. Lord, I can't

You said: "He who is not for me is against me"

Right!

What about the wounds you receive in the house of your friends?

settle to any work. Stop me from worrying, make me trust in you, and, please, keep her safe. And make her come back soon before I go out of my mind.

Indigestion prayer

LORD, I have indigestion and I am miserable and bad-tempered. I could snap anyone's head off at the drop of a hat. Lord, it is utterly stupid that such an ordinary complaint should alter my whole outlook on life. No doubt you are right to give someone like me such a humiliating affliction! If you won't cure it, could you help me to live with this discomfort a little more cheerfully? And show me how to choose what I eat more wisely in the future.

Hay fever

I'VE tried to make every sneeze a prayer. Every time I've blown my nose I've said: "O Lord." Now my eyes itch and my throat irritates, and my head aches. I'm still sneezing and wheezing. What a funny man you've made, Lord! I can't ever really enjoy your sun and green fields. But sometimes when I feel you in the middle of this, Lord, I can love and laugh and know that you were a man in dusty Israel, and thank you, Lord.

Why do you allow hay fever, Lord? It's such a stupid sickness full of irritation and sneezing, headache and wheezing. I suppose it is just because it is so stupid, it is a good one for me—keeps me humble and makes me see how easily I snap at people. And when I cannot breathe, sometimes I manage to realize the wonder of breathing and the taste of fresh air. How odd this very richness of your nature!

Cheerfulness

LORD, keep me cheerful even when everything seems to be going wrong. Give me such a sense of your love that I will always appear joyful. But don't let me become hearty and annoyingly bright when the people I'm with are miserable and want gentle and understanding love.

Putting off writing letters

LORD, I am putting off writing letters today, telling myself tomorrow will be time enough for them. Lord, I know this is wrong but I can't bring myself to get down to writing. I'm always putting off things like writing letters and visiting people. Help me, Lord, to summon up enough energy, enough will power to do things when they should be done, and not leave them to tomorrow when I probably won't do them anyway.

Work

DEAR LORD, give me the grace to do my work with all the ability I possess however humble it may be. I could easily do it carelessly, with half my mind, for no one would notice, but it is what you have given me to do, so I must do it well. Help me to keep this in mind when men run down the humble jobs of the world and to remember that when your son worked quietly as a carpenter he was doing your will in the same way as when he was on the cross.

Noisy neighbours

LORD, my neighbours nearly drive me mad with the noise they make. I can't understand how they can endure their music so loud, I can't! Could you please make them realize how I feel about noise, and could you make me control myself sufficiently to go and talk to them calmly about it. Show me them as people, individuals, who have likes and dislikes like I do. Help us to see each other's points of view, and that by so doing we may work out a way of living peacefully and companionably as neighbours.

LORD, you tell us to love our neighbours. I suppose I try to, but mine are so noisy! Just when I am going to sleep at night, they start apparently moving the furniture around. If we want a quiet talk in the evening, they put the TV up to maximum. When it's summer, they play a transistor in the kitchen window, which is wide open. Lord, stop me from being noisy back or hating them. And would you help them too about loving their neighbour?

Taking in a down-and-out

LORD, he came at eleven o'clock tonight. He smelled of booze, he was ragged, and filthy, and reeked just of human dirt. He said how cold it was, and I wanted to

46

shut the door and say no room. But they said that to you, Lord, and somehow I couldn't. But, O Lord, what shall I do with him tomorrow?

Apologizing

LORD, teach me how to apologize gracefully and not grudgingly when I have done something to cause another hurt or inconvenience. Often I can't bring myself to apologize at all, even when I know I have done something wrong. It needs a kind of courage and humility which I seem to lack. Please help me to break down my pride or any other barrier that prevents me from making this gesture of repentance which I know is important in human relations, and in my relationship to you.

Being in love

LORD, it is utterly wonderful being in love. The whole world looks different; it is transformed, joyous, and shining. I cannot thank you enough for letting this happen to me. Never let me fall out of love. I know the way of loving must change, must deepen, perhaps even become less obviously joyful, but please make it endure. Help me always to be considerate and understanding, and stop me from causing pain to the one I love. I ask this in the name of your son, Jesus.

Let me love her properly

LORD, if I am honest, I've got to say that a part of me,

a large part, wants something to happen with her tonight. You know I think I love her. And I know there is a lot of sex which is only partly love. So my prayer, Lord, is all mixed up. I suppose it is: "Let me love her properly and let her love me. Don't let it go wrong, but let something happen which is all right." O Lord, I'm torn. Be with us.

Let me love him properly

LORD, I love him so much that I could throw myself into his arms. And Lord, if he wanted me to sleep with him I'm afraid I might, though I think it wrong. Lord, give me strength to do what is right, and make him understand my point of view. It is hard being a woman in a permissive society! Other girls in love give everything and I seem so unloving and ungenerous. O help me, Lord, to do right.

When an affair ends

LORD, my girl has given me up and I am utterly miserable. Please help me to know what to do: should I try to get her back or should I simply accept the situation? Whatever I do will be painful, and I need your help badly. I am very lonely without her and keep remembering the things we did together, and the knowledge that we won't do them again makes the past joy bitter. There seems nothing left in life. Help me not to be disillusioned, but to keep on and to live in hope. I know that you understand and will always love me no matter how much I grumble about the things that you allow to happen.

I was in love, Lord, and she said she loved me. Now she says it was all a mistake and there's someone else. I still love her, Lord. Help me not to hate her—or him. Help me to understand and to show I love her by letting her go. Oh, God, it's hard!

Problem of an older person

LORD, help me to know what to do. He said he'd sleep in the sitting room, but he is in her room now. I know that they are going to get married soon, but by my interpretation of your gospel they are doing wrong. Lord, is the charitable thing to leave them be or should I express my view? You would have known how to correct them gently and lovingly, but my approach is clumsy and heavy. Anyway, Lord, bless them and keep them, and I do thank you that they love so much.

At a wedding

LORD, help me to pray now for the happiness of the bride and groom, and not to look around to see who is here, how they have changed since I saw them last, and what they are wearing. Stop me from hoping that the service will be short because my clothes are tight and uncomfortable. Lord, make me keep praying that the couple will always love each other and that their love for you will grow. I'm worried that they are getting married in church because it is the thing to do. Lord, speak to them now so that they may come to see that you are in every situation of their life, both in joy and misery. Amen.

A parent's prayer

LORD, how can I trust my child to that man? She is my daughter and has been for eighteen years. I love her so and don't want her hurt. Lord, I can't control myself and I want to protect her—but wouldn't that be wrong? She must be herself. She must choose, and I must sit and watch but I mustn't interfere. Lord, give me strength to go on, and not to butt in and want to possess. Lord, help me really to love.

Coming to manhood

LORD, I don't know much about you, or if you really are. How do we know? But there is one bit I read. It said you "were subject to them." As a young man I find being subject so hard; I rebel all the time; my parents often seem stupid and out of date. I want to love them. I think I do. But let them accept me as a man, Lord, not treat me as a child.

Growing up

LORD, growing up is bewildering and wonderful too. I long for something or someone but I don't know for what or for whom. This longing is painful, but I sense that it is possible to attain to something which is beyond all dreams. There are so many things I'd like to do. I rush to do them, but then become afraid, afraid that, perhaps, I won't be capable of doing them, afraid that the achieving will be disappointing, less than the striving and dreaming. Lord, give me courage to go on searching, don't let me become disillusioned; help me to find someone whose love will fulfil me and whom I will fulfil. Always be with me in my searchings and my findings, and let me see you in the midst of them.

Visiting the old

I'M GOING to visit an old lady, Lord. I know what she will say, because she always says it, like a poor old broken record stuck in the same groove. And I'll feel like giving her needle a shove, Lord, only I mustn't, must I, because she is not a record but a person, built in your image, loved by you. Give me that patient love that you have shown all through history as mankind goes through the same groove of faithlessness and failure.

LORD JESUS, I am going to visit an old lady who will tell me the same stories all over again, and I will have to look bright and interested. It will be very dull. Please prevent me from showing my boredom, or from making clever remarks at her expense. Help me to become interested in her as a person; give me understanding of her problems; and show me how to be patient and understanding like you. Lord, also, let people who find me dull and boring be patient with me in a similar way.

It's all very well saying
"FOLLOW ME"

but
where
on
earth
are
we
going?

LORD, I've been visiting a very old lady and she was wonderful. She was interested in all that is happening around her and in the world. Though she enjoyed the enthusiasms and liveliness of youth, she was content to be immobile and crippled herself. She seemed to trust and love you completely and this somehow made her love and take an interest in me and my friends. Lord, help me to learn to trust and love the way she does, for I so often waver in my belief in you and in others.

Fear of hurting other people

LORD JESUS, you told us most clearly the penalties we would have to pay if we hurt the babes, the little ones of the world. Lord, I am very afraid of hurting sensitive people and those with tender consciences. I can do this so easily, and the hurt can go so deep and be so lasting. Lord, save me from this, for I dread doing it more than almost anything else.

A difficult person

SHE's your creation, Lord, and if you don't mind me saying so, I can't imagine why you made her that way. She's unattractive, she's boring, she's a menace. I can only pray that you will take her out of my life. I know that's not nice and not charitable, but I can't take any more of her . . . so what, Lord?

LORD, he is unbearable and infuriating. He exudes masculine pride and thinks he is irresistibly fascinating!

He talks me down and I only think of bright remarks later. He needs to be told he is not always right! His vanity is so great that I can't make him realize that I don't want to see him again. Lord, can't you penetrate his thick hide and make him leave me alone? And you would help womankind if you could deflate him a bit.

Respect for others

LORD, teach me to respect people, to accept each person as unique and created by you. Some people seem so unattractive, twisted, prejudiced, self-centred and demanding that I want to avoid them. I find it extremely difficult to see you in them. Help me to treat them with the consideration that I would like to receive from others. If I could see myself as others see me perhaps I would be less critical and more understanding, so please help me to do this. And of your goodness give me compassion for myself and for others, and never let me give up trying for the sake of your son who genuinely loved and cared about sinners and outcasts.

Prayer of the timid

LORD, help me for I am timid. I cannot say the things I'd like to but simply remain speechless in company. You have given me talents, good qualities, but they have to stay hidden because of my shyness. I love you and would like to reveal something of you and your goodness to the world, but this is difficult since, being tongue-tied, I seem so stupid. Lord, help me to be the person you'd like me to be. Perhaps you want me as I am, if this is so I am content.

Sleeping in a strange room

IT's a new bed in a strange room, and I'm restless and can't sleep. Everything goes around in my mind as I toss and turn. Give me the grace to relax, Lord, to lie still in the darkness. Teach me to pray and not to worry. It is your night and I am yours; your will be done.

Rushed meals

LORD, thank you for a wonderful meal. It's marvellous to have time to eat slowly. Normally I eat in a rush in messy coffee shops, and have no time to enjoy your good gifts which don't seem at all good in such surroundings. Lord, help me to organize my life better so as not to rush so much; further, perhaps, I would have time to see your goodness in creation and in others.

Doing something new

IT's very scary, Lord, I've never done it before. I don't know that I can, so the whole of me is empty inside and almost sick. I'm a coward, Lord, but you said: "With me all things are possible." Give me strength to go through with it, hearing you say: "Fear not."

Listening to a dull preacher

I CAN'T help it, Lord! Every time he opens his mouth in the pulpit, I begin to doze off. He's hopeless, Lord. Oh, I'm sure what he says may be right and true, but it is dead, and it's killing me. Would you ever think of sending your Spirit on him . . . on me, too?

For a strong faith

LORD, people expect me to trust you completely and not to waver in my belief. Dear Lord, I am very often helpless and lost, but know I must rarely show it as it might cause those who are less strong than I to weaken. Strengthen my belief, increase my love so that I may be a support to those you have given me to help, for without you I can do nothing.

War

CAN'T you stop this bloody war, Lord? If you can't, I don't know who can. And if you don't want to, I can't see how you are good. It's up to you to show me, Lord. It's more than I can grasp.

How am I responsible for war?

LORD, why do you let men fight wars? Why do you allow labour camps and concentration camps? Why are men brutal to each other? What has made us like this?

Lord, I suppose I must be responsible in some way for the hate and horror there is in the world, but how, for I don't want things to be like this. Show me how I can help to change the hearts of men. And change my heart, too, Lord, and make me a little more understanding.

Before study

LORD, help me to concentrate on the work that I am about to do. Don't let me fritter my time away with idle thoughts, and help me really to get into things instead of just learning superficially. Keep my mind open to the thoughts of others, no matter how different from my own. You understand everything, everybody, and listen to everything. Help me to be open, more like you; make my understanding and sympathy more like yours.

Emptiness before an examination

I SIT in front of my books and I turn the pages, but nothing seems to go in. I'm frightened, Lord, I don't know what is happening and I am losing my grip. There are exams coming and I can no longer learn or think, and I've lost confidence with people, Lord. I can't even make friends. But, Lord, you can help me find myself and my friends and my work again. Send me your spirit of understanding and love.

Examinations

LORD, I am getting panicky about my examination,

worrying whether I will get the kind of questions I can answer and whether I'll have time to finish the papers. Please calm me now and make me more trustful and content to leave myself in your hands. I know I should not be upset, but I am, so please give me the ability to let go my worries and to rest peacefully in you, my Lord and protector.

During the examination

LORD, the time has come and I don't know anything. I think I worked, but it has all gone out of my head. Help me, Lord, give me calm and help me remember that the results are in your hands; that, whatever the outcome, *that* is the best for me and, mysteriously, for your kingdom too. Guide my thoughts and my words, and give me the peace that only you can give. I put confidently into your hands not only this exam but all my life, which I know to be deep in your love already.

Prayer after failing an examination

LORD JESUS CHRIST grant me the grace not to brood over this failure but to accept it as your will for me at this moment. Let it be a means of increasing my knowledge and love of you, and of making me better able to bring you to others. Teach me to be, in my innermost thoughts as well as in my words, gladly aware, now and at all times, that I depend completely on you.

Lord, you know I have failed, and you know how frustrated and disappointed I feel; for though I knew

You came to set prisoners free.

Lord, set your people free.

it might happen—and, perhaps, ought to happen—I still hoped. But I know this is part of your plan for me; other doors are open, help me to find which door is for me and to go through it with courage. Thank you for this, make me accept it with love, and thank you for all your surrounding, everlasting love.

Prayer of a theology freshman

LORD, hurry to my assistance—I need your help! Help me not to be distracted in my prayer; how often does my mind wander when I should be paying attention to you!

Help me to concentrate on my studies; let me listen to the teacher who teaches me your ways. Teach me patience and tolerance and do not let me be disturbed so easily. Teach me to be cheerful and amiable, and do not let me think uncharitably of my colleagues.

Only on you, O Lord, should I centre my thoughts. It is you I want to serve; it is your priesthood I want to share. Lord, I humbly ask you to hear me.

Prayer of an alcoholic

GOD save me! I'm an alcoholic, and I know I am. I fight it; I say I'll cut it down; I do a bit, but then I start again. Lord, it's so hard, at these moments of tiredness and depression, to get over the next hump. Only you can give me strength. I'll try again. Lord, give me strength.

Beginning a new life

TOMORROW, Lord, I am beginning a new way of life. It's a step forward into the semi-known and the unknown. It asks for far more trust than I have, and, Lord, I am afraid. Give me courage and openness to go forward in trust and loyalty and love into your world which is also mine.

Silence and daily life

LORD, by knowing you in silence and stillness, I come to perceive you working in hidden ways in my life, in the circumstances of daily existence, and through others. It is very mysterious and wonderful, so please help me to keep attuned to you in daily life so that the business and noise may not separate me from you. Let me always make my life a prayer to you. Help me to find you in every event, so that my prayer and my life become a unity flowing in and out of each other.

The wonder of God

LORD, you are wonderful and all I could possibly desire. The perception of you, which is both darkness and light, remains always with me, though you so often leave me when I just seem to have found you. I both possess and lose you; you draw my affection but do not satisfy my full desire. Give me more of yourself and the strength to accept the dangers which come from living close to you, for you are a purifying and consuming fire, and it is very terrible to fall into your hands, but it is only there that I find peace!

V

"When" Prayers

When tired

LORD JESUS, you were tired, but were you ever too tired to care? Lord, I am so tired that I can hardly keep going. Give me strength to keep on peacefully so that I do not snap at the people about me, who do not know how I am feeling. Give me your kind of strength which in weariness still thinks of others, and when night comes give me peaceful rest in sleep, and I'll try again tomorrow.

WHEN you came to the well in Samaria, you were tired, Lord. Yet you immediately opened up to the woman and gave her both deep instruction and careful, tender counselling, so you won her and others, Lord. Now teach me how to do this when I'm tired; how to keep interested; how to let another talk and give myself in tiredness so that I may give you.

When sleepy

I WAS wanting to go to bed, Lord, and then he came in to talk. He went on and on and now I've missed an opportunity because I didn't really listen, I felt so sleepy. I was glad when he went. Let him have learned something, Lord, received some help, and teach me patience and interest. Amen.

When worried

LORD, when I am worried help me to come to you and to lay my problems before you. It is very easy for me to brood this way and make my distress worse. Teach me to hand myself and my worries to you so that they don't escalate. Let me continually hear you saying: "Peace be still," so that I may be calmed and become more trusting, for the sake of your son and our Lord, Jesus.

When bored

I AM thoroughly bored, Lord. There is nothing particular I want to do; the ordinary daily round is dragging and dull. I don't want to look into the future, because it all seems so tasteless. There is emptiness in my mind and heart—a dryness that nothing waters. Give me the patience to go on, Lord, till there is a breakthrough, and if you don't want it that way, so be it.

When life is bewildering

LORD, the way is very dark; I do not know what the future will be, nor what you want me to do. Please give me the faith to trust in you and let me always remember that I am supported, protected, and led by your love whatever happens. Help me to realize that you will give me sufficient light for each day and that you know where you are taking me; make me content to live in the present moment for as long as you wish.

When I take myself too seriously

LORD, when I am taking myself too seriously, make me look in a mirror so that I can see reality and not the fine image that I create of myself. Help me to laugh at what I see and to stop being self-important and dramatic. Make me remember that there is laughter and joy at the heart of the universe as well as sorrow. Let me acknowledge my weaknesses and learn to enjoy the absurdity of myself and of the world, and, Lord, when I become too intense, don't take me seriously either!

When at breaking point

I CANNOT understand how anyone can go on under this strain I have at home and at work. It is worry all the time. More bills this morning and we no longer seem so close. The office is hell, Lord, all tense, grinding hell. Don't let everything break, Lord. Give us strength and peace to find our way through.

For trust when things are difficult

LORD, teach me how to trust and obey you, for I am certain that this is the only way I will know real peace.

I find it difficult to trust and to walk calmly among the pitfalls of life, as I know so many dreadful things can happen. It is only with the strength and love that you give that I can believe good will come out of the bewildering and painful events that befall me and others. Teach me, as you did Job, to say believingly that even if you slay me yet will I trust you. I ask this for the sake of your Son who trusted most perfectly.

When I want reassurance

LORD, I try very hard to do things for other people, to be helpful and loving, but I often wonder if people notice. Is it wrong to want sometimes to be told that one is useful or kind? It is very hard, Lord, working in a vacuum: I am confused and don't know whether I am doing your will or what people want me to do. I think you expect me to go on blindly, but could you not let me know sometimes if I am doing the things that please you?

When I listen to others

LORD, help me to listen patiently and understandingly to the people who want to talk about themselves. They have troubles and joys which mean so much to them and so little to me. Stop me from interrupting them unnecessarily. Don't let me talk about myself, pretending it's important. I can't forget myself but at least let me be a loving listener, and help me to give truthful advice tactfully.

When I speak without thinking

LORD, I so often speak without thinking—words come rushing out. Frequently it is fascinating gossip which makes people laugh, but if repeated could be hurtful to those it's about. At other times I am critical in a clever way that can make people curl up. Lord, words can be used in so many good ways but I am expert at using them cleverly in my efforts to amuse. Teach me not to speak without thinking. Show me when it is discreet and merciful to be silent, and when it is right to be critical and angry.

When I am not understood

I DON'T think he really understands what I am trying to say and do. Now Lord, you know how hard it is to make people understand. They didn't understand you, I know, and yet you remained so gentle and kind and understanding. Please teach me how this can be done. And if it is possible for him to understand a little, then that too I ask.

When driven mad by in-laws

LORD, I could easily give up! My in-laws are always fussing around. They watch what I do and usually it's wrong. They criticize. They interfere with the children and say I neglect them if I allow them to play on their own. Lord, I could scream and tell them what I think of them. I can't take it much longer. I'd walk out if I didn't believe marriage is for life. I've no one to go to but you, so please help, make something happen to keep them away for a short time at least! Give me a strong and persistent love. Goodness knows, I need it!

When depressed

LORD, I am depressed. I have lost my vision and life seems meaningless. I don't know where I am going, and I can hardly keep on. I would like things to be different, but I am not sure how. I wish I was somewhere else, that there was someone to turn to, that I felt you near me. Lord, I know that these are the circumstances that you have given me and that I must live with them, but it doesn't seem humanly possible. So, please give me vision again and a sense of purpose. Make me realize that you are with me when I am depressed, guiding and helping even though I may not know it. I ask this for the sake of your Son who also knew the misery of human frustration.

When flustered

LORD, things are going wrong, and I am becoming agitated, and may say and do things that will hurt others. Please help me to trust in you and keep calm. Make your peace well up in me and still my agitation, so I may behave as you would have me do.

When I am intense

LORD, I become too intense about the many things which I care about passionately and so I often put people off them. Help me to be less ponderous, less obviously concerned. Stop me going on and on when they lose interest. Give me lightness of touch and the sensitivity to know when it is right to talk seriously, lightly.

When emotional

LORD, I am very emotional and often become too involved. I've got caught this way again and the complications this time seem unending. But you must know what you want of me, for you created me, so please get me out of it without hurting people too much. And next time show me more clearly how to control and use my emotions.

When I am callous and hard-hearted

LORD, help me, for I am callous and hard-hearted. When I hear thousands have been killed in an earthquake or flood, I think to myself, "Good, that will be less to feed in an overcrowded world: if people breed like rabbits, nature will inevitably even things out." Lord, help me see the afflicted as people who love, hate, and fear as I do, as people whom you love. Soften my heart, and make me care a little for the distress of their families and friends.

When lonely

LORD, I am very lonely. I don't know what to do about it. I realize that loneliness should give me a chance of getting to know you better, but how do I start making you my friend? Could you, please, encourage me to respond to your love and help me to realize your closeness all the time. I find this hard to accept in daily life though I believe it in theory. Could you perhaps send someone into my life who knows how to talk to you so as to tell me how to begin to appreciate and perceive your nearness to me at all times?

When afraid of being a fool in public

I'VE got this thing, Lord, about being a fool in public. It just gets me and it is so silly. It wastes time and gets me all hung up. I can't open my mouth for fear of being thought a fool. And if I'm silent it is just as bad. Sometimes it seems they are all looking at me, as they did at Peter when he denied you. I feel like running away and hiding. Give me the courage to be myself, Lord.

When afraid of doing the wrong thing

YOU said: "Don't be afraid" to your followers, Lord. But I'm always afraid of being different, of doing the wrong thing. Perhaps the worst fear for which I want your help is the fear of doing what I sense to be right when it "isn't done" or when it will be unpopular.

You did not hesitate, though I think it cost you a lot. Give me the openness just to be before you, and the courage of the convictions which grow in me. Help, Lord, for I have little faith.

When self-sufficient

LORD, I am not often afraid and I can persist at things. Lord, it's so easy to be proud of these abilities, to think I am responsible for them. This makes me independent, makes me think I don't need others, or sometimes even you. Those who are afraid learn to rely on you and to trust. Lord, I want to trust and be yours to forget myself, but I keep on being made to do things myself, and not to expect help from others. Lord, I'd much rather be dependent and trusting; won't you send me circumstances which will help me grow in reliance on you?

When self-conscious

LORD, help me to lose my self-consciousness and to become centred on you so that I forget myself. Keep me from retreating into my shell when people do not respond to me. I react too quickly to other people's attitudes, take on too easily their mood. Please anchor me so firmly in you that I forget myself. Live in me and be the motive power of all my actions and reactions, so I may respond to others as you would have me do.

When hurt by a friend

LORD, I've been hurt again by my friend. I mind so very much and would like to give him up, but I know you want me to keep on loving. If I disobey you, I turn away from you and in some sense lose you, and who else have I to go to but you? I can't leave you—so, Lord, please help me to go on loving whatever the cost, and give me self-control and wisdom.

When I have hurt a friend

LORD, I have just hurt a friend. In a way I didn't mean to do it; in another I did it deliberately, for I am tired, fed up with the demands made upon me, with never having time to myself, and I wanted to let off my frustration on someone. I can't be angry with the bewildered or distressed who come to me for help, but surely I can let go with friends? Make them understand this, Lord; help them to forgive me and not to hold it against me or give up loving me.

When told off

LORD, I've been told off! I know I was in the wrong, but this makes me all the more angry and annoyed. Give me strength not to swear back, but to accept the telling-off with outward calmness. Also, Lord, don't let me sulk or look disagreeable. Help me to ask forgiveness of you and of others whatever I've done wrong —but just at the moment keep me silent!

75

When snapped at

LORD, I have suddenly, unexpectedly, and unreasonably been snapped at. I would like to retaliate. Lord, don't let me be bad-tempered. It would make things so very much worse. Help me to be self-restrained and good-humored, and for heaven's sake bring things back to normal, quickly if possible, before I explode.

When jealous

LORD, I am jealous. It is hateful, uncomfortable, and I feel ashamed, but I keep on feeling this way. The one I love seems to be more concerned with someone else than with me. I don't know what to do; I am so hurt. Please help me. I realize that I should go on loving and not hate, that I should love you with all my heart and others in a lesser way, but it isn't working out like this at all. Take me and work in me with your love so that I will be able to love and care for people in an unpossessive way. Lord, it is good to talk to you and to know you understand and forgive me, for I don't want to be jealous. It just seems to happen. Please keep supporting me so that I may become more like you.

When I want to help others

LORD, I want to help the poor and those who are suffering, in the kind of way that you did, and not in the condescending way do-gooders are condemned for.

Give me the ability to see you in the lowly of this world and to love them as you do without thinking of the cost to myself. Let me learn from them in a humble way, and then surely I won't be condemned as a do-gooder? But if I am let me see you in my judges.

When criticizing others

LORD, never let me forget my own faults when I begin to criticize others. Stop me from judging people harshly, and make me remember that they have the same kind of temptations as I have. When I sin, I plead the circumstances of my life and my nature as excuses to you; help me in a similar way to excuse the faults of others so that I may become more tolerant and understanding. Help me to forgive the wrong which people do to me and to those I love, in the same way as you forgive me, for the sake of your Son, who on the cross forgave his executioners.

When deaf

LORD, I am getting deaf. Not hearing what people say, not knowing whether they hear what I say, makes me feel cut off. I am becoming more and more isolated, driven into myself, and it is lonely, for I enjoy people so much. I feel so stupid too. Lord, help me to look happy, not miserable, for this puts people off from making even a small effort to communicate. Lord, don't let me be permanently deaf, for people are not very understanding of the deaf!

When acting as peacemaker in the family

LORD, it is very hard being the buffer between my husband and the rest of the family. The task of peacemaker is without honour; both sides think I am taking the other's and both abuse me. Lord, help me to continue to try to keep the peace, to try and make the views of the middle-aged comprehensible to younger people, and to interpret the younger to the older. I see the virtue on both sides; please let them see this too. And, Lord, give me the strength and patience to keep going and not to give up.

When a good and useful person has died

LORD, why have you let (insert name) die? He has helped so many people and could have been useful to so many others. I just can't understand why you take such a person out of the world and leave so many who spread destruction or lead empty, useless lives. It doesn't seem to make sense! I know your Son had to die in order to be raised again, but (insert name) and his work will simply be forgotten. What good can come from it? Can't you show us something of your over-all plan so that we can understand a little better your incomprehensible ways?

When trying to understand God's ways

LORD, you do seem to make some odd mistakes: you let such strange people have power and important jobs, while your friends are kept in obscurity. It is very hard

for us to understand your reasons. I know we only see
a small portion of your over-all plan and our perception is limited, but what you allow to happen does
seem very odd. It would help if you could explain
things to us, but we might not understand even then;
nevertheless you could try; perhaps you do and we don't
notice for our eyes and ears are closed. If this is so,
open our eyes and ears so we can perceive a bit more.

LORD, why do you ask so much of us? Why should it be
so hard to follow you? Why must we leave the easy life
for you when you seem so far away and unconcerned?
When you give me glimpses of you, I understand a little
better; much, so much, of following you is sheer grind
and seemingly profitless. Give me faith to keep trying
to follow you and strength not to give up.

LORD, there are many things on your earth which I
don't understand, but one particularly worries me: why
do so many people, who are not Christians, live good
selfless lives when numerous people who profess to be
Christians and go to church are so unkind and unchar-
itable? Does it make any difference whether we believe
your Son was God, believe in you? Am I wasting my
time trying to follow Jesus?

When trying to understand pride and humility

YOU know, Lord, I think I could run the church and
the country, and even the world, better than they do!
And I sometimes feel I could do it better than you!

Pride, pride, pride! Yes, but that is the way I am, and, in the past, it has helped to get things done. Is it all bad, Lord? Or part good? Help me to get the measure of pride and humility.

When getting older

LORD, now that I am getting older, help me to accept the fact that I cannot rush about as I used to do, but have to take things more easily. Make me realize that I can still do what you want just as much as before but in a different way, and that by smiling and talking kindly to people I am serving you as much as in the days when I worked more actively. Help me to remember that you want me to go on slowly and steadily in a relaxed way and that now, as in the past, I rest always in you.

When the telephone rings

IT'S that telephone, Lord! Every time it rings, I fear the worst—those endless conversations, that trapped feeling, the inadequacy of anything I can say. Then, too, that irritation at being interrupted, that snappy desire to hang up, that tendency not to listen. With all these things, help me Lord. That telephone may be a life line for those who ring, a voice in despair, a note of love in loneliness. Amen.

When I want to tell others about God

LORD, I want so much to bring people to know you, especially those who are bewildered about themselves and the meaning of life. But Lord, I don't know how to begin to do this. I know the wonder of you, the joy of life lived with you, but how can I explain this, show this to others? I become tongue-tied, and can't find words when I try. Lord, help me to forget myself and my inadequacy. Act through me so others may come to know and love you. I ask this in the name of your Son.

When I see God in my muddled life

LORD, my situation is muddled, complicated, difficult, but now I suddenly see your hand in it so it is not completely black. Somehow you are guiding me, strengthening me in a way that is almost imperceptible. I realize that I need adversity so as to come nearer you and to grow as a human being. The pain, the darkness are still real but the sense of you being in it too gives me a glimmer of hope. Keep letting me know you are there, for the sake of your Son Jesus who remained faithful in great darkness.

When I have drunk too much

LORD, you gave the wedding guests wine in Cana of Galilee. Lord, I have had too much to drink. I know I will regret it and will be unable to work as I should. Please forgive me for having loved your gifts too much.

VI

The Modern World and Its Problems

Living with noise

LORD, help us to come to terms with the maddening noise of town life; the noise of cars, motorcycles, planes, factories, trains, the blaring of radios, televisions, and hi-fis, which deaden our ability to think and to savour life. Enable us to shut this out and to build an interior silence in ourselves where we can meet you. Also give us opportunities to be alone and quiet, so that refreshed and with our faculties sharpened, we may return to live at a deeper perception and at peace amid the noise.

My neighbours

LORD, help me to understand and appreciate my neighbours whose colour and way of life are different from mine. I know that they are men and women like us, your children too, but they so often act differently from us that I find this hard to believe. Their cooking smells different, they chatter loudly, they are so noisy that it is hard for me not to complain about them. Help me to understand their way of life, and see the good things in it, and by being tolerant come to love them for your sake.

Prayer of a black person

GOD, it's awful to be black in this country full of white people. It's not that everyone is unfriendly, though some are. It's just so different from home—ideas, ways, talk, laughter. I'm an alien, an exile, however much I try. And then sometimes, Lord, they seem to hate me, and then I hate them back for all their superiority and whiteness. Lord, help me to understand and be understood. Amen.

Cultural barriers

LORD, help me to understand people who are different from me, people who have a different way of life whether they are black or white, Russian or Chinese, or simply coming from other parts of the country. It is hard to appreciate their customs, their food whether it be tortillas or pizzas or gefilte fish. Colour and language make the difficulties clearer, but it often isn't easy for a Northerner or a Southerner or an Easterner or a Westerner to appreciate each other. So help us to break down any barrier which keeps us from your children who are different from us.

For courage in a permissive society

LORD, I am afraid of being laughed at because I want to live as I think a Christian should. Never let me give up trying to keep your laws however people may mock. Never let me laugh at people who are trying to do right. Lord, it is not easy being your disciple in a permissive age when conformity to permissiveness is the law of so many. Give me a clear vision to see what is right and the strength to do it, and take away my fears.

Save us from hell

LORD JESUS, we are constantly shown on TV, in the newspapers, and in the movies the horrors of the world, the evil and perverted behaviour of mankind, so that we come close to despair. You, Lord, in your life knew failure, saw men betray and torture each other. You knew hell on earth as we do, but you did not despair, for you loved men and trusted your father. Keep alight in our hearts the flame of hope, make us to see the beautiful and good things in the world, not just the drab, the squalid and sordid. Help us to see the goodness of men, and by our love increase this and make it grow and spread among the people, for we are your instruments in the world. Make your hope and love shine through us so that the hells of others may be lightened and they may glimpse something of your glory.

Make me free

LORD, people are always talking about freedom, about being free, but I find it very difficult to understand what true freedom is. Doing what I want the whole time doesn't seem to be true freedom; if everyone did this life would be chaotic. Help me to discover what freedom is. Does it come from forgetting myself and serving you and others, since I am told that in serving you I will have perfect freedom? Help me, Lord, to live in such a way so that I can be freed of my own selfish desires which imprison me more than most things I know.

I'm all caught up, Lord, in what I am. They tell me, the learned men, that everything is determined and I have no freedom. Sometimes, I feel this, but yet, deep down I know I can be free, with the freedom of the sons of God. Release me unto myself, Lord, release me unto the world. Let me be real, let me be free.

A happening

I'VE just been at a rock festival, full of youth, noise, and rhythm. I know quite well it is "not me" and so some of me rebels against it. At the same time, I feel its life and its soul expressing so much that young people are and want to be. Lord, give me the openness to make the kind of relationship with them which brings them into being.

For a sense of correct values

LORD, there are so many wonderful things nowadays,

cars, refrigerators, TVs, hi-fis, tape recorders, and the like, that we can easily get too preoccupied with them. Our values can so quickly go wrong. We can forget that people are much more important than things, and that the spiritual part of our nature can get so stifled by exclusive interest in material things that it withers and dies. Lord, it is particularly easy today for us to gain the whole world and lose our own souls, so please keep alive in our hearts the love of you and our neighbours.

Life in an affluent world

I LIVE in an affluent world, Lord. Whenever I read about the difficulty of the rich man getting into heaven, I wonder about me. I'm rich, Lord, not only in material things, but in faith. Dig into me, Lord, if this is what you want, then make me give my goods, my time, my love, myself. I'll not give, if you don't push me, Lord. I need your strong example to live in me.

Are men on the way out?

I WENT through the power plant today, Lord. It was frightening, so few men about, Lord, just metal and steam and valves and pipes. Are men on the way out? Is it all to be computers and machines? Where are we going, Lord?

For perseverance in our work

LORD, give us perseverance and help us never to give up

when our jobs are difficult or dull. Make us realize that, though keeping on and keeping on with drudgery is hard, we grow and develop by doing this. We won't get to heaven driven in a Rolls-Royce, but have to plod uphill on foot. Help us to see that the journey can be invigorating and companionable if we share the difficulties with you and with others. Lord, teach us how to persist, and not to be put off by problems or by boredom, but to face up to them as your Son did, and keep going on.

For courtesy in a busy world

LORD, show me how to be courteous. It is so easy to be concerned with my own activities that I forget to treat people with care and consideration. I rush about on my business, have no time to hold doors open for the heavy-laden, for the old and infirm; I push past others so as to get to my destination quickly. Lord, help me to be considerate and polite, for this can mean so much to others, for the sake of your Son who was kind to the weak and despised.

For drug addicts

THOUGH it has not happened to me, I know and love some to whom it has happened, Lord. They are yours and they are my fellows, but they have drifted on to drugs. There are so many reasons, Lord. You know them, I can only try to sense them. They are shy, they are weak, they can't communicate, they're misfits, their homes don't work, they want to belong, they want to be loved, Lord. Give them your understanding when we don't understand them: give them your strength when they feel the craving; above all, let them feel your love in you and through us. Help them, Lord.

Have you forgotten us?

IF YOU really created this world, why is it all such a mess? Have you lost control, God, or don't you care any more? You say in Scripture that if the mother forgets the young, you won't forget us. Well, today she often does. What about you, Lord, what about you? Have you forgotten us?

VII
Marriage Prayers

Newly wed

WE ARE just starting out together, Lord. We only married a few days ago, and now I am back in our apartment, our own first home. It's everything, Lord. He's gone off to work, and I must go out soon, but I wanted to spend a moment just relaxing, and looking and tasting the joy of it all . . . with you Lord, quietly. Jesus, you knew what it was to love, though perhaps not quite in this way, because you weren't married, were you? But you kept loving, ever more deeply, even when you were abandoned. Oh Lord, I want to ask now that you keep us from ever abandoning each other or you. Please let this wonderful love go on and on and on. Never let it get tired or droop. Never let it look anywhere else for satisfaction. Please let us love each other till death as we are, and not falsely; let us love each other in our children, if you bless us with them (and, please do!) ; let us love each other in and through you. Lord, let us keep and develop the freshness and youth of our love each day, always. Amen.

O LORD GOD, it is incredible to be in love! Thank you for being love . . . thank you for creating the possibility of loving.

LORD, help me. I love her so much that I want to keep her all to myself, yet somehow I feel that this isn't the right way of loving. You, who love us so completely, don't try to possess us. You have given us freedom; freedom to choose what we want to do, freedom to grow in our own way. Prevent me from trying to possess her and from trying to make her into the kind of woman and wife I think she should be. Lord, help us both to love for each other, for others, and for you. Don't let either of us stifle the growth of the other by possessiveness.

LORD, I love my husband very much and I know that he loves me but when I see him talking to a young and attractive girl, I get all tense and worried. And I let him see this and he doesn't like it as he thinks I don't trust him, and that I am always watching him. It's just I love him so much, Lord. Please help me to trust him more, and if I get worried at least stop me from showing it.

LORD, help me to know and understand her better. She is wonderful to look at, her face seems to me to reflect the wonder of her experience of life and its beauty and her mind is alive and sparkling with interest in people and in your creation. She is so wonderful I want to explore all of her, body, soul and mind; help me to do this gently and tenderly. And, Lord, let her get to know me too, the best and the worst of me. Make her tolerant and understanding of the worst in me. Lord, I don't want to hurt her but I am so imperfect that I do and say things I don't really mean. Help us by loving conflict to become the kind of people that you want us to be. Lord, don't let me spoil her spontaneity and joy in living. Let us come to know you more clearly through loving you more deeply and so be more fulfilled as people.

LORD, he loves me so much and this gives me a great sense of joy, but also of power because I can so easily get him to do what I want. There are so many feminine wiles a woman can use to manipulate a man who loves her and they are exciting to use! O Lord, I know how it is to use this power wrongly though it can also be used in a right way. Make me think seriously about my motives before I try to influence him, and don't let me simply play games with him and his love. Help me, Lord.

LORD, I haven't had much to do with men before. I never really knew my father. I'm discovering how different a man's attitude to life is. I love my husband, but he makes jokes in a very simple and direct way about sex and things I trust with respect and delicacy. I'm finding it hard to understand and not to be shocked. I don't want him to think I'm puritan, but I can't understand how he can be so insensitive to my feelings. Help me, Lord.

Loving when tired

LORD, I'm tired tonight and my head is aching. I just want to go to sleep, but he is very loving. I don't know what to do; should I tell him how I feel? Somehow it isn't easy and not really right. And when I've done it before, I've usually regretted it. I don't want him to feel rejected after his miserable day. Lord, help me somehow.

He's infuriating

LORD, he is quite infuriating. I've taken great trouble in fixing a meal for him and it was really good. But he's eaten it almost in silence and now he has rushed out to be with the boys. When I said, "Isn't it good?," he ate even faster and said, "Oh yes." Give me patience and help me to understand him. And, Lord, I would like a little encouragement.

Temporary estrangement

LORD, we are treating each other like strangers and we are both miserable, at least I am and I'm sure he is too. I am not certain what happened, but we were both at fault. Now we smile politely and talk to each other in a stilted, bright way. Our relationship seems to have frozen and have no life. I think he is furious with me; if only he'd argue or tell me off, perhaps we'd come alive again. I don't know what I am supposed to have done, but Lord, help me to apologize in the sort of way that will restore our love and sense of companionship again.

Onset of alcoholism

LORD, I never thought you would let married love be like this. I love him so very much, and up till now, everything he has done has seemed wonderful to me. Today, I know he is an alcoholic. I've seen him drink, but I never guessed. Today, I know; the doctor told me after he crashed the car. He's all right; he's alive; but, Lord, what happens next? I still love him so desperately. Will this kill my love? How can I help him? I am so very ignorant and feel quite inadequate when he has had too much. Guide me, lead me, teach me to live with him in strength and love.

Thanks

LORD GOD, I want to thank you for married love and for the gift of children with whom we can share and live and grow that love. Oh, I know it isn't easy all the time, and there are days when I get down and depressed. It is strange, really, how at these times, it is easier to share with those down the block or at the club than it is with the one I love more than all. Don't let that always be so; teach me to share sorrow as well as joy, and to take his sorrow and his care on myself when he asks me to do so. But right now, I want to thank you because you showed me the way when you lived at Nazareth. There you made me see the patience and understanding of Mary, who took those things she did not understand and pondered them in her heart . . . and that through this it was possible for you to "grow in wisdom and grace before God and man." I'll try to be patient; I'll try to understand; I'll try to ponder when I don't. And as of now . . . thank you again, Lord, for what I know so far of married love.

Prayer together for the children

THE children are in bed and we are praying to you together, Lord Jesus. We love them so much, and we want them to grow up all that you and we would want them to be. We thank you for them, Lord, but we want your help. Because we love them, we are so terribly afraid. The world all around is so full of danger and vice. There is mugging and hijacking, murder and theft. Keep them safe, Lord—at least it is not quite "keep them safe" . . . it is let them live and grow and not be "got at" by the world. You see, there's an extraordinary mixture, Lord, in this creation of yours. There's generosity and selfishness, love and hate, goodness and evil, hope and despair, gentleness and violence. Give us the strength and joy in believing to help them to love and serve you positively, and to love you in their neighbours. Make us and them really Christian, Lord . . . and no! don't exactly keep them "safe," but please keep them for yourself. Amen.

LORD, we ask you to protect our children who have

gone out into the world to live and work on their own. We trust them and we've tried to teach them to love you, but now they are mixing with cynical, unbelieving people who will try to undermine their faith and their Christian approach to living. It's like seeing small boats start out in a rough sea and not be able to protect and direct them in any way. O Lord, give them courage to hold on to their beliefs and standards of behaviour, and to give us more faith in you and in them.

When my children are growing up

I WANT so much to let my son and daughter grow into real, mature people, Lord. You went through this growing up, and somehow Mary and Joseph knew how to be there and to give you the relationship of love and trust and strength you needed. Help me, Lord, to be all these things they were, so that my own children may be man and woman in their fullness.

Children

LORD, we married because we loved each other and we wanted to be together and to grow together, and so in your time to extend our love in our children. We really wanted this, Lord, and we always believed that this was the fullness of married love. But you haven't allowed us any children, Lord. How is that? Are we on the wrong track? Or don't you trust us or what? We've tried to love you and serve you. Oh yes, we have failed again and again, but surely you don't hold that against us, Lord? So what is wrong? We have prayed and taken advice, and done all we were told by doctors, by friends, by priests. Nothing—Lord God, help us! Make us fruitful. It is not too late. Lord, hear our prayer— and make it soon, O Lord of Life.

Death of a wife and mother

IT's terrible, terrible, Lord! How can you let this thing happen to us? We married for love of each other. We pledged ourselves till death . . . but we never thought it would come so soon, this terrible separation. But you have taken her away; you have allowed her young body to be eaten up with cancer, and she's dead, Lord; my lovely, happy, beautiful one is dead! How could you, Lord? Have you no pity, no mercy, no love? And what about the children? Am I now to be father and mother? The kids aren't even old enough to help themselves. How can I get on without her? I simply cannot see. Surely I'm not wrong to ask you, because you made us and I believe you love us, and right now I can't see where love can come in to what has happened. How can I feel your love for us in this parting, this death? God forgive me! I don't mean to get at you, but I can't help questioning. Please—guide my thoughts where they can't find the way, guide my actions where they don't know the way, and guide my heart where it has lost its way. And, don't let the kids suffer, because I really love them, and so did she, and they are ours, and she is still about in them. And I believe in the resurrection too, only not very strongly just now, and I beg you to let me really believe and to sense her closeness, her life, her love through being with you in prayer and the Eucharist. You see, I feel so very much alone as I struggle on without her physical presence. O God, I'm so lonely and lost. Amen.

VIII

Prayers About Illness and Death

When in pain

LORD, I am in great pain. Help me. I need you to prevent "the thing" from dominating me, absorbing me, enclosing me. And yet I know that in my pain I am more closely united to the refugee with his cholera, the wino, the mother who has lost her child, and all who suffer, since in suffering all are united to you suffering on the cross. And because of this I can only say, not my will but yours.

Praying when ill

LORD, now I am ill I have plenty of time to pray, but I am too taken up with my pain and fears to do more than say, please help me to endure, don't leave me, and remember me when I become so concerned with myself that I forget you. Help me to put myself in your hands even though all I want to do is to complain and resent the suffering.

Hospitals

LORD, I hate hospitals. I hate the noise. There is no privacy. I'm just a back, or a leg, or an arm, and I can make almost no decisions. But, Lord, I know absolutely that I am here for your purpose. Help me to see you in the pain and frustration as well as in the loving care.

Before an operation

JESUS, I am very afraid. I do not know what is going to happen to me. I have absolutely no control of what happens and I dislike not being in control. I am afraid of the loss of consciousness that the anaesthetic will bring. I worry that I will be a burden to others after the operation and that I will not be able to be as active as I was. Lord, help me to trust you. Arrange my life even though it may mean "my being carried about where I have no wish to go" (John 21:18). Let me realize if I die now I will be coming to you whose love casts out fear.

Sleeplessness when ill

LORD, I can't go to sleep, and there is nothing I want more. I want to escape from my difficulties and yet I know that with your strength the waking time can be most precious, your God-given time to pray for all those who in the hours of the night are lost in darkness. Take this darkness from them so that they may know your light.

Impatience with illness

LORD, I am never patient. Impatience is part of my nature. Yet, again and again all through my life you have eventually granted my prayers. Help me to ask always that my petitions be granted in your time, not my time.

Complaining when ill

LORD, I am sick, in pain, heavily drugged. I want to accept your will, and yet when anyone visits me I am tempted to complain endlessly about what is happening to me. Lord, help me to break through this barrier of self, to be alive to the interests, troubles, and, above all, the sufferings of others.

Fear of death

LORD, I am ill and I don't know what is wrong with me and no one will tell me. Lord, help me for I am afraid of dying; afraid that I will cease to be and that the world will go on as if I had never been. Ceasing to be after the fullness and joyfulness of living is a terrifying thought. Lord, I am no longer sure that I believe you exist, or, if you do, that you love and care for me; yet I think I have experienced your love, come to know you in prayer, but here I am back with my childhood fear of ending in nothing. Please give me a firmer belief and a deeper knowledge of you so that I may trust that when I die I will come to live more fully with you than I have ever done here.

Lord, you did not seem to want to die—at least not that way. You did ask your father, they tell us, "let this chalice pass"—but he didn't and I can see why. But "this chalice," Lord, my chalice, my sickness which they won't tell me is my dying but which I half know and half dread—if only, if only. There is so much I still want to do, Lord, and I'm afraid. So help me be calm and help me say "but not my will but thine be done."

Convalescence

Lord, for weeks and months I have been helpless, being washed and fed, amused and spoiled, now you are beginning to give me back your gift of health. Give me courage to use your strength to take each step as I am asked, patience to be as slow as you want me to be, daring to go faster than I feel I can go, and above all help me to forget myself, the fussed-over and petted invalid, so that I may become again totally given to you through others.

When friends are dying

I KNOW he is dying, Lord. I've known for weeks, but we talk and pray and even laugh and plan as though he was getting better. It all seems such a lie, so false. But should he know? I don't think he does know; the doctors say: "Don't tell him." But he loves you, Lord, and perhaps he would serve you more and love you more if he knew. Lord, let me understand what I should do.

SHE is dying now Lord; she's no longer conscious. But it may go on for hours or days or weeks. Help me through, Lord, and also give me strength just to sit and be with her, though I can do nothing for her, except pray. Though I love her, it is so easy to get up and go away, so hard to understand what you are at, my God. Take her or make her better; don't let her just hang about. Yet somehow this must have a purpose, which I don't see—so your will be done. Only, if it's not cheating to ask, do it quickly!

LORD, help me to understand why you let people linger between life and death so long. This waiting is hard for us and for them, yet it may be important to you. Are you working on them, purifying them and us? A friend suggested that it was at such times that you unravelled the knots and tightnesses which grow in us, and that such waiting was right and good. Could you please help me to see a little of what you are doing when situations seem simply futile and useless to us?

Trying to understand suffering

LORD, it's not easy to understand suffering. I rebel at it in myself and in others. But I've met a man who has

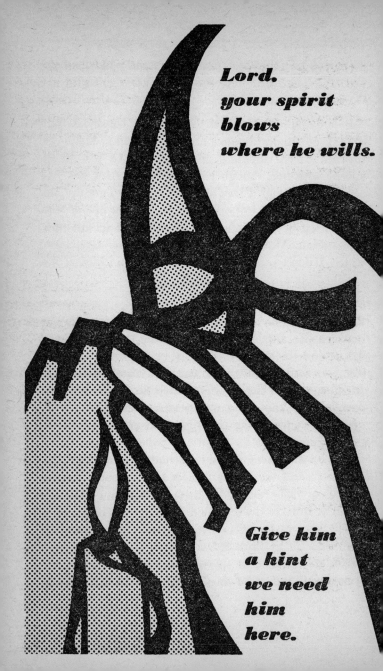

been suffering intensely for years. I sat by his bed and he almost writhed in pain—and he was cheerful and full of hope, and he said: "How good God is!" Well, Lord, who am I to complain then? Thank you for the lesson, Lord.

Death in an accident

WHY, oh why, Lord, did you let that happen? Why let that fool crash drunkenly into him and kill him? Have you no pity?

The death of a child

LORD, you gave, you have taken away and I am trying to bless you! It is very hard, I miss him so much, and I am so lost. Help me to be able to give you eventually the love which I gave him, and ease my desolation and loneliness now. Stop me from reproaching you and from wanting to curse you, and answer in some way or another my question "why, why, why?"

LORD, he was only two, and you had to take him. Why, Lord? I can't think why you let him be born, just for this. Poor little fellow, he knew nothing but pain. He suffered and so did we. Why did you have to be so cruel? What is it all for? Can't you see how it is destroying the little bit of faith I have? . . . and yet, Lord, if you aren't there, and no one cares, however strangely, why should we go on at all? Even at the very bottom of this bottomless pit of sorrow, the only hope is in you. Somehow, against all sense, I grope for the fact of you. I know I don't really understand, but please teach me at least to be unselfish, not to hate his death because I miss him, but to accept that he is happier now than I could ever have made him, and that I'll be with him again . . . but Lord, I still wish you hadn't let it happen that way. Forgive me for being so selfish!

Death of a young man

HE was only young, Lord, a student at the university. Everything seemed to go for him, youth, good looks, intelligence, charm. He had a lovely fiancée, he'd landed a good job. Often he spent his free time caring for down-and-outs. Then he was dead by the side of the road, his friend's car wrapped around a tree. Why, Lord? Anyone else—but why him, Lord? Why?

IX

Prayers About Prayer and About God

Help my unbelief

I SUDDENLY thought—supposing you aren't there, Lord! What then? Could it be true you don't exist? Well, yes, it could! I know that, and yet, and yet . . . Lord, I believe, help my unbelief.

Difficulties and doubts

LORD, forgive me when I doubt the divinity of your Son, Jesus. People try to make Jesus so human, so like us; they obscure all his hard sayings; they forget how often he filled people with awe and how his disciples frequently failed to understand him. Lord, help me to realize how much there is about him that I do not understand; help me to penetrate more deeply into the mystery of his being and so learn more about you and about myself. Help me to realize that though my mind may not grasp his significance, by love I may come nearer to understanding the mystery of him and to know that I will never fully comprehend the richness of his being.

When it is hard to pray

LORD, I am trying to pray but I am without any sense of you or your presence. I do not want to be like this. Please help me to continue praying however dead I may feel. I am not even sure that I want to pray; make me keep on trying, and in your good time give me a sense of your presence. It is so hard to continue without it, and I am very weak. I do not think that I can stay this way much longer, so please help me soon, dear Lord.

LORD, it is so difficult to start praying that I want to get up and leave. Stop me, make me stay. Lord, blanket the thoughts about my daily life which keep running through my mind, and let me know that you are close. It's wonderful when I feel your love in this way. If this is not right for me today, give strength to stay put with you in darkness and help me to know you are as much in this as in the warmth and light.

I JUST sit here, Lord. It is very strange, because I want to come to your house and pray. I really look forward to it. And then when I come it's all dry and shifting. I'm frankly bored and restless. Somehow, Lord, I suppose I understand but it is really very odd—a bit of nonsense to my mind. If it is really your way of leading me on, so be it. But if you can give me a glimmer, thank you, Lord. And really when I leave your house again, I know I'll want to come back.

It's no good

I'm empty

I'm bored

I don't really believe

So if you are there
do something

Please !

A sense of sin

LORD, I am weighed down by a sense of sin. I cannot separate out specific sins, but I know my strivings for you can be half-hearted, all my good actions can be spoiled by mixed motives, and even my purest love may be tinged by self-indulgence or possessiveness. Also I keep wanting to see if I am improving and becoming holy, not because of you but for my own self-satisfaction. Lord, I hate my half-heartedness, my half-giveness; make me forget myself, my self-interest, and look only at you, and let your will become the ruling force in my life.

Give me a vision of you

LORD, open my eyes so that I may see you; open my heart so I may experience your love. My eyes will be blinded by the vision of you, and my heart will be overwhelmed by the fire of your love. Let me not be afraid of dying to myself so that you may become my vision and the be-all and end-all of my life.

Self-offering in prayer

LORD, I am silent before you and I offer myself to you; do what you want with me. Help me to be open when you speak to me in the silence; keep my mind quiet and my body relaxed, so that I may truly be still and know that you are God, know that you are all that I could possibly desire, and know the wonder of your love, my Lord and my God.

Lord, my love makes me speechless before you. Accept this dumb gift of myself.

Take me over, Lord

I REALLY want to give myself, Lord, yet so many things hold me back. First it is this and then it's that, but always something. So I know, in my heart, that it is simply me. I get in the way, I find excuses. Cut through me, Lord, strip me of all this selfish self; fire me a little with your generous love—in fact, take me over. I am yours, and I'm afraid and already I am holding back again, so take me over, Lord.

The wonder of God's love

YOU have done so much for me, loved me so much. I wish I loved you more and could show it. What can I say or do? When I feel your love, it is as though I would burst into laughter and achieve anything for you or anyone else. It can pass all too quickly, and in fact I don't live up to what I want to do for you. But it is wonderful all the same, this strength and power, this serenity, this depth. Even when I fail your love, your love doesn't fail me. Oh, for an unshakeable love like yours, which would go out from me to you, and to all those I find so hard to love who are round about me.

Let me not possess your love for myself

LORD, in prayer, you have let me see and know you and

your love in a most wonderful way. Lord, forgive me when I think I deserve such vision and knowledge, and when I try to possess and keep them for myself. Rather than this, Lord, let me go into the darkness which is beyond the realm of sense. Also let me accept as your gift the desolation of heart which must be part of my life until your love and beauty are revealed to all men.

Desire for God

LORD, my desire for you is insatiable. I long for you, and to see and know you more fully. This desire torments me—you let me glimpse you and then you desert me. I do not know what to do, where to look for you. I need you more than anything else, the half-remembered love is not enough. Lord, I am no poet, no artist, I cannot cry to you in heart-haunting words as others have. My love and desire make me dumb; I can only say: Lord, come and never leave me!

To the Holy Spirit

O COME, Holy Spirit, inflame my heart, set it on fire with love. Burn away my self-centredness so that I can love unselfishly. Breathe your life-giving breath into my soul so that I can live freely and joyously, unrestricted by self-consciousness, and may be ready to go wherever you send me. Come like a gentle breeze and give me your still peace so I may be quiet and know the wonder of your presence in my being, and help diffuse it in the world. Never let me shut you out; never let me try to limit you to my capacity; act freely in me and through me, and never leave me, O Lord and giver of life.

HOLY SPIRIT, come like a mighty rushing wind and awaken us out of our complacency, our apathy, our indifference. Stir us up, disturb us, for we are too content to let things go on as they are, and to let people go on not knowing you. Awaken us to a sense of urgency. Penetrate the closed gates of our hearts and make us live again. Make us struggle with the problems around us, for in this way we will grow and develop while in our apathy and complacency we slowly die. O Holy Spirit, create among us a mighty Christian revolution; and cast the fear of the unknown out of our lives; make us realize that however impossible a situation may seem, your strength can remove mountains.

To Jesus

LORD JESUS, you are all I want and I find in you more than I could possibly need. Lord, though I know this now and swear that I will never leave you, yet I realize I will go searching after other things in order to fulfil my never-ending wants and desires. Fountain of everlasting life, spring up in my heart and satisfy all my needs so that I will never wish to leave you again.

X
Intercession

Help me to ask in faith

LORD, teach me to ask in faith. I pray for wars to cease,
but I am half-hearted because I don't believe man could
stop being greedy so I think there will always be war.
I pray that people may become more loving and tolerant to each other, but I don't really think that they
will change. I pray for people to recover from their
illnesses, or if they don't that they will grow more like
you and will learn from their pain, but I ask half-
heartedly, not believing. Lord, increase my faith in you,
in your goodness and love, and help me really to believe
in your power to work in others and in myself. Save me
from being cynical and give me faith as a grain of mus-
tard seed which will grow and flourish. Jesus, I ask this
in your name.

For those I love

LORD, I pray for those I love. Keep them safely. Give
them your peace. Help them to love you more and to

know that in every danger they remain in your safe-keeping.

Praying for others as they are in themselves

LORD, help me to pray for people not simply as they affect me, but for them as they are in themselves and in relationship to you. It is so easy to ask you to make them love me, treat me with respect, and find me interesting. Lord, help me to see them as people who also need love, respect, and interest, and forgive me my self-centredness. Be in my relationship to them and bring us close to you.

Prayer for the busy

LORD, please bless and help people who are so busy working for you that they can find little time to pray. Give them strength to keep going and a sense that you are always with them and in their work. Help them to realize that others, who have more time, pray for them and what they do, for in such ways we share with you in the bearing of each other's burdens.

For those with unpleasant work

LORD, help those who have unpleasant and unrewarding work, those who are weighed down by great responsibilities, and those whose life is full of disappointment and who have little hope. Lord, strengthen them so that they may bear their burdens bravely, and when possible give them companionship so that their loads may be lightened by being shared. May our prayers and those of the saints be a help to them, for they are made in the name of your son, Jesus, who carries the burdens of the whole world.

For the distressed of the world

LORD, teach me to care for the suffering and distressed who are close to me, in my street, in my village, in my work. Show me how I can help them. Teach me through their misery to appreciate the sufferings of those in distant lands who seem so remote and difficult to pray for; help me to perceive the wonderful bond of love that links Christian people with all mankind and which aids us in bearing each other's burdens. Make us more loving and considerate to each other, O Lord Jesus.

For an alcoholic

HE's an alcoholic, Lord. He knows it, and so do I. Of course, he does try, but he's so weak. I wish I was always there to help, but I am not. Can you help, Lord? Will you help, Lord? He is so good and he does try, but we all know he is going to fall again. Help, Lord!

For understanding those whose ways of loving differ from mine

LORD, help me. It is very silly of me but I am filled with

revulsion and draw back when I see women holding hands and gazing at each other affectionately. Lord, help me to understand their need to love and be loved. Give me your spirit so I can live more tolerantly.

Lord, I have been brought up and lived with such a view of morality that I have always thought of homosexuals with distaste and even loathing. Now I feel that I must somehow grant them the charity and justice they deserve; but I still can't help feeling a great revulsion. You know, Lord, I think deep down I despise them, and despise myself for doing so. Please, make me more open to your kind of loving, make me appreciate them as really human persons, with their burdens and their loneliness and their need of love.

Lord, so many of us are narrow and bigoted, especially about sex. But when we swing the other way, we seem to lose all sense of balance, and just become permissive. I don't see how we can keep straight and broad and wise and loving unless your Spirit leads us. You alone can give the true love which we are told is patient and kind, understands everything and bears everything. If only we could be like that! Lord, send your Spirit into our hearts.

For those who are without work or insecure

LORD, assist those who cannot find work, and all those who are in any way insecure. Send people to help and strengthen them, but best of all help them to solve their own problems. Show us how we can be of use, for so

many restrictions seem to hinder us. Often we are afraid to become involved, as we want to preserve our time or money for ourselves. Give us a persistent kind of love so that we will find a way to help whatever the difficulties.

For a teen-ager in prison

HE is in prison for life, Lord! In a way he has never had a chance—no parents, no home, no love, no God. Then he was in trouble, and on the run he killed a man . . . breaking in, Lord. He was hungry, you see. So what now? He knows the wrongness and regrets it deeply. He's been to the pit of despair, and now he's hunting for you, Lord. He wants you, and he wants to build anew, to know, to love, and to live. Give him the courage and strength to live in that beastly place without further damage; give him light and hope and patience to go forward. And, Lord, give me the wisdom and warmth and patience and love to help him. Amen.

For a man in prison

LORD, he is rotten and vicious and lying and unlovable. I find it very hard to go on visiting him inside. And it's the same when he is out. So little hope, Lord, and such a chip on his shoulder. Somehow he doesn't care; he's got no respect for himself; he doesn't want you or me or anyone. Yet there somewhere is a lovable, touchable human person. Let there be a breakthrough and a softening so that he can come out next time and live.

LORD, he has just gone to prison for six years, and he has asked me to pray for him. I don't know how I should pray. I realize that he deserves punishment, but being cut off from his family is very hard and won't do him any good. Help him, Lord, in his loneliness. Keep him from becoming a subhuman creature that just lives, eats, and sleeps, or from becoming embittered and full of hate for the world. Lord, give him some interest or occupation that is creative and let him know that others care and are praying for him. And show me how I can help, and how I should pray for him.*

For those trying to help the downtrodden

LORD, strengthen those who are trying to help the apathetic and who are struggling for the underprivileged and discriminated against. When they seem to fail save them from bitterness of spirit, from cynicism, from loss of faith and hope, and when they have success give them humility. Encourage them always to be bold and patient, and fill them with the joy and love which the gift of your Spirit brings; make them realize how much they may learn from those they try to help.

Intercession for hippies

LORD, I pray for the hippies, the drop-outs, and all

* This prayer was written at the request of a priest who had been asked to pray for a man just going to prison. He was at a loss to compose a suitable prayer and he could not find one in any book of prayers. "In the end," he said, "I said the Lord's Prayer for him."

those who are disgusted by the materialism of today. They seem to be searching for the meaning of life, and for you, though they may not know it clearly. Help us, who try to serve you, to show them the way to you by being self-giving and self-sacrificing. Keep us from being smug and superior. Give us your grace so we may "live loving" as they try to do, and so in this way may be able to guide them to Jesus, who lived completely loving.

Deep intercession

O GOD, you have poured into the depth of my being the pains and fears of those for whom I pray. It is draining and consuming. I shudder and tremble. My body cannot bear the weight of the oppression. Lord, I don't want to be exhausted, for I have work to do. I don't want people to see me looking tired. No one would believe that this dark shapeless prayer is work which I do with you. I know that the helplessness and lostness will continue with me throughout the day. I try to get help from others for the bearing of this burden; I look for reassurance but I do not get it in any obvious way, though underlying the pain I know a strange peace and strength, which you and those that pray with me give. Have mercy, Lord, and leave us not comfortless.

O LORD, it is terrible when you take me at my word and let me share the pain of the suffering in prayer. I am overwhelmed and driven to my knees. I twist and turn, but there is no escaping it. I can get help from no one; you too seem to have left me. Is it like this for those who despair in loneliness, for those who, trying to escape by way of drugs, are drained of life and vitality and sink downward? Lord, have mercy on us, support us, and let us see that in the end "all shall be well, all manner of things shall be well."

For unity

LORD, I feel very deeply my separation from other Christians when I attend their Eucharist and cannot receive Communion. Why must we be so cut off from each other at the moment when we should be sharing you? This should be the time when we are closest together, but it is now that I know most deeply the agony of separation. Lord, if it breaks my heart in this way, how much more must it break yours? We love each other and we love you; why must we be separated at this feast of love and union? Lord, make it possible for us to worship together in complete union and fellowship, and show us what we must do to bring this about!

XI

Praise and Thanksgiving

THANK you, Lord. It was wonderful! I got completely caught up in beauty and love and joy. Oh, let it happen again!

Lord, I want to praise and thank you for the joy, the love, the beauty you give us. I thank you for the sun and the sky and the whirling, billowing clouds which I see above the grey, sad houses of the town. I thank you for people who understand about you and your love, who understand when I haltingly explain the wonder and joy of you that can be found even in pain and suffering. I thank you for ordinary people who catch the light and spark of your Spirit, who though they live in dingy surroundings give us a glimmering of your love. I thank you for the wonder and beauty of ordinary things; please keep our eyes open so that we may appreciate them and thank you for them.

I'm caught in this, don't know quite what. I'm bubbling, Lord, with a sort of below-the-surface joy, an inner laughter. Carry me along, Lord, and let me somehow share it so that we can sense your promise: "Your joy will be full."

Are you playing the fool with me, Lord? I ask because I am so happy. I want to thank you for everything, but why do you do it? There isn't any reason for your goodness to me—I've done nothing to deserve your love and care. But thank you, Lord, and I'll try to trust and not wonder all the time "why?"

Thanks for being able to live in the present moment

LORD, I thank you for teaching me how to live in the present moment. In this way I enjoy each simple task as I do it without thinking that I must hurry on to the next thing. I do what I am doing with all my ability and all my concentration. My mind is no longer divided, and life is more peaceful. Thank you for teaching me how to do this, and please help me how to show others the way to learn to trust you more completely and to do everything which has to be done at your time and for you.

Thanksgiving for compliments

DEAR LORD, thank you for people who say kind, complimentary things. I keep on trying to do what I think you want of me; I can't see that I am doing anything very well. I get tired and depressed and wonder if I am doing right, then someone compliments me, says perhaps, "It's good to see someone looking happy," or

Lord. I am hopeless.
so sinful.

but I do love you.

So please help me.

"What you said helped me." Some small, unexpected compliment can change my mood, encourage me, make life seem worthwhile, and even make me love you more. Lord, bless those who help people in this simple human way. Lord, help me too to praise and compliment others spontaneously and naturally, for doing this can make their lives happier, as well as encouraging them.

Thanks for letting me experience your love

I was sitting there, before you, Lord, and I was quite dry and empty. It was hard even to stay put. And then quite suddenly, I knew your love. Somehow, it filled me, warmed me, wound me round and made me come alive. I just went on sitting, but it was . . . and . . . is quite different now. So, I just want to thank you. And I want to say that I think there will be a time when it is all cold and dark and blank again, but that even then, because I know your love, I will trust and be thankful.

Thanksgiving when things are going well

Lord, I am always running to you when I am distressed and in need, so now that everything is going well I would like to thank you for all you have done for me and for giving me so much joy. I also ask your forgiveness for the times I fail to thank you rather like the healed lepers in the Gospel. Help me to bring all my life and its events to you so that I can share them with you and so come to know and love you better.

Thanksgiving for finding God in unexpected places

LORD, I find you in so many places that I marvel at the wonder of your ways. Help me to learn to expect this and not to be surprised. I have found you in the sacrament on the altar, in the sick and suffering, in the wildness of the hills and the sea, in the preaching of your Word, in ordinary kind people, in flowers and trees, in small children, and often in events, in trivial events which lead me to people in need. In the sharing of their problems I may have given help but also I have found you in them giving me new vision, new peace, new courage. This finding of you is wonderful but it is demanding and it seems that I have to give as much as I receive, and you keep on asking for more. Teach me to understand something of the economy of your kingdom so that I may not be totally overwhelmed by its unexpected interchanges.

Thanksgiving for peace

LORD, I thank you for the peace you give us when we let go our worrying, forget our self-concern, cease our rushing about, and rest in you. This wonderful peace fills the whole of me and overflows into the world. It makes me love you and those around me in an all-embracing way. Lord, help me to be self-forgetting and never let me try to possess this peace for myself, for, like your love, it must be continually outgoing.

XII
Night Prayers

LORD, my thoughts are going round and round in circles. All the activities of the day crowd into my mind, and jumble and jostle each other. I am far from peaceful and am quite uncomposed for sleep. Could you, please, calm me, the way you did the storm by saying quietly: "Peace be still"? Lord, give me your peace, your deep peace, so I may sleep restfully and get up tomorrow refreshed and ready for another busy day.

DEAR LORD, this night I commend my spirit into your hands. All my desires and petitions are open to you. You see all the good I wish for those I love and for the whole world, and the thanks I'd like to give you for the past day. You know how I try to love you and I know how your blessing enfolds me at all times, and particularly now when I fall asleep, leaving my life and my friends peacefully in your care.

When sleepless

LORD, the night is coming again. I know it is your night, but I get so depressed and don't even feel you about. No one cares. The clock ticks on so slowly. I cannot sleep. If only I could pray or share with others, or feel wanted. But I can't, Lord. Please, at least let me sleep!

LORD, here I am again awake in the night with pain gnawing my inside. I don't know how to lie so as to ease it. Please give me strength to stay still and not to twist about and make it worse. It's a bit like being very hungry. I know it's a chance to share the pains of the starving of the world, but I don't seem to see it that way. Help me, Lord. Let me sleep, for I've so much to do tomorrow and I want to wake refreshed.

LORD, thank you for letting me know your love as I lie here sleepless. Often I lie in darkness of mind and soul unable to sleep or to find you; tonight I can only say thank you for this deep peaceful joy, and ask that you will give me it again.

YOU know what you have done to me, Lord? When I wake up in the night, even before I am fully awake, there is a glow of peace and joy. And then I'm lying there awake, and I know your presence. Somehow it doesn't matter if I sleep or not. To sleep is rest, to lie there in the dark is quiet joy. Thank you for this, and help all who suffer sleeplessness in the same way. Your love is much better than a sleeping pill.

148

XIII
It's Me, O Lord

IT's ME, O Lord. That really is all I can or need to say. But sometimes, I just want to go on talking to you, because I feel hurt and alone and neglected and lost. It helps then to sit and tell you that it is a very self-pitying me who looks at you and sometimes wants to curse you and run away and hide from your anger. Then part of me says: "If you really loved me, you wouldn't let these things happen to me," and I feel all curled up in misery, empty and unloved. You know, I even think you hate me when I am deep down like this, Lord. But then there are other times when everything is wonderful. Then I just want to sit and say: "It's me, O Lord . . . and thank you, thank you, thank you" . . . somehow just to say it once isn't enough, and I have to go on and on. And then again, there are times when I am just there, and I know that you are just there too, and it seems right to say: "It's me, Lord," not because it's necessary, but because I am me and you are you, and after saying this, there remains the wonder of you and the nothingness of me; the glory of your creation and the deepness of knowing what it is to love and to be loved by God and man. It is you, Lord, who makes this be; it is me and all your creation in which it can be and is. Thank you, Lord, for everything and everybody, and most of all for being you and being there always, but most consciously when I say: "It's me, O Lord."

Index of Subjects